What Lies Behind

What Lies Behind

Luann Hiebert

*Blessings as you continue
living the WORD.*

Luann Hiebert

Sept /17

TURNSTONE PRESS

Turnstone Press
Artspace Building
206-100 Arthur Street
Winnipeg, MB
R3B 1H3 Canada
www.TurnstonePress.com

Turnstone Press gratefully acknowledges the assistance of the Canada Council for the Arts, the Manitoba Arts Council, the Government of Canada through the Canada Book Fund, and the Province of Manitoba through the Book Publishing Tax Credit and the Book Publisher Marketing Assistance Program.

Printed and bound in Canada by Friesens for Turnstone Press.

Library and Archives Canada Cataloguing in Publication

Hiebert, Luann, 1960-, author

What lies behind / Luann Hiebert.

Poems.

ISBN 978-0-88801-474-0 (pbk.)

I. Title.

PS8615.I362W43 2014   C811'.6   C2014-901260-8

for
Terry

Contents

What Lies Behind

look who's looking

in the mirror   I see
my mother see she
     grows in my face
     shows her face
looking back at me/me
looking back
     speckled green eyes
     face spattered with soap
        filmy spots
        freckles speckling

spots in the mirror
     dabbing on makeup cannot
     make up for the time
being
     our reflection
     the flecks
          of my mother
          mother of me
          /me a mother
     reflect on
     mom/me
          how un becoming
       I am not (I am
becoming

tracing

tongues of snow blow.
swirls and piles
wedge into cracks
melt under the door

a blue line of tracks
foot-on-foot trace
through piling winters

mother's blue prints linger
in the silent flurries
impressions stashed under
the doorframe of my mind

      her handy woman ways
doing laundry
an old ringer washer
      lines of diapers
      flapping in the stark sun
zippered red hoodies sewn
      for daughter and sons
staking faith
      in tomatoes and beans
seeds grown for her own
      seedlings despite
      the bite of winters
drifting duties
      fill the cracks of childhood
her hands
      tracing snow in the bank

sun flowers

trees stand
    still
northern poles
against icy sun
rays arrested
   light
       freezes
their tracks
stems sun
-scalded brown

time stands stark
grows white in the heart
winter's em
brace   sun-sparks
our tongues
sap flagging
lungs burn breath
caught cold
love-hold of un
spoken desires

        a stand
      of contraries
    a December daze
is our polar burden
       the sun
      hesitates
       its stiff
    light chills

    a freeze-dried sun
its brown love brittles
   flowers in your
     mouth still
      you I love
   not with standing

hoar frost

you catch my
breath
your breath
catches
on the line

you defy gravity
hold on
telephone
wires puffed
white with delight

your beauty
burns
my eyes

crowded stars
flare
on the line
your frost furs
every thing

my mind wired
to your
snow song
your wraithed
charm

breath-burrs
glisten limbs

I live on
the line
tickled pink
by your spectral
hold

it's got to be

the right shade of blue
a hungry sky

the right amount of spice
in the simmering stew

before he comes
home it's got to be

the ripe hour of twilight
when linen lies

smooth to touch & welcome
we fold into each other

in the evening-hungry sky
it's got to be

the right shade of blue

sour apples

blue light sags
beneath
       unwieldy branches

            (*autumn's*
             burden)

unfit for pie
sour apples
      mouldering

            (*autumn's*
             blessing)

      provender
fit for winter's
foragers

           (*so sour &*
           oh so sweet)

the morning after

it has come to this
the morning after
    sheets chilling

morningale sounds through snow
blown streets warming
    her window café
hums brimful

honey-grain biscuits brewing
coffee to shiver away the storm

shadows sweep her away
    crumbs a-drift-in
    a winter mind field

thought I saw you

thought I saw you
today
      veer past
      in a deep
            red van
      your face
            sun struck

just for a moment

thought I saw you
today
      jump off the page
      imagined we turned
            a new leaf
            stirred ink blots
erased
      we were
      living grape vines
            climbing brick walls
               growing clusters of fruit

thought I saw you
today
      in the jewellery I wear
      thirsty for you

thought I saw you

           exchanging glances
              face to face   blind/sided
              in the morning mirror

poems out of line

out of line
the cord lengths of words twist in
                                   & out of line
                      swing in the wind like a school girl

~

how long does it take
to turn the line

                the time it takes to puncture skin
          zing the mind out of time through the eye intra
                    -venously
the arterial motives vital
      to turn
               toward e/merging bloodlines

hung out to dry

out of line
hung out to dry
her poems hang
on the line
fresh & wet
words pinned
on hangers strung along unseen wires
seeking sun
that will bring them

the whole scene a flapping frenzy
she hangs out
(this preposterous poet)
these laundered luanndering lines
publicaly
extravagantly
shamelessly

de-arranged
completely out   of
line

lining

hand-stitched with care
& silky smooth she wears

her coat of many colours
lined & buttoned
                    to the page

to make a bee line

how to make
            a bee
            line straight
            when bent utterly out of line

            string a line from here   to   h o r i z o n   & run
sunhot well-shod
                        shot with good intentions
                        warm up & hit
                                    a line drive through the droning hive
                                    smack into the honey sac

                        buzzzzzz   buzzzzz
                                    bzzzzzz
                                                zzz

spell-bound bee
            take a direct course
            of course see that you don't   get off course
                                            get lost
                                            get left out
                                                        hanging mid
                                                        -flight & far a
                                                        -field

                        like fallen pollen & land
                        just short of the bee tree
                        like Luann & her
                        last bee quest

drag on fly

               flit   & fly
             little dragon
                  fly

          wing   &   drag
          on the grey-faced
                 sky

          draw your name in
                       pen
             -sive
             lines

          your quad-quills whirl
             iridescent miles
                                dart in/
                 visible
          calligraphy   in flight
                rag   on
                       gravity

15

glory-drawn

the sun
           well-seasoned pinches
eyes blind   the shine
sweet ginger   smacks
          your line of vision

the traipsing breeze
bumps & pings against
tree leaves
         rings your ears

catch earth's praise   the days
            perfumed with birds

            joy beneath your wings greens

drawn to your palm
a fly iridescent
        spies a vagrant crumb
            tongues its way
to sweet treasure

in the distance
        a car engine
revs anxiously on its way
to God knows where

much as you
try to catch today
by its whirring tale
                the buzz & hum
      glory-drawn

prairie

prairie   airy   pasture
   purple clover   prayers
   windy   fielded sea
                           grain gold

rare   fair   reverie
   savoury grasses

buttery   fresh   moon
   thunder blitz lightning
   northern sky flicks
                          night shades

garden   seed   granary
   rains   reaping praise
   bearded wheat bread
                          grape wine

landscape of home

a coyote howls at the splash of moon
echo echo across the grass & stone
     his voice answers
     the sound of silence
               is anyone there? there?
               does anyone care? here?
a vast & blackened space
night-emptied of company

paled by the dripping moon he calls calls
to the purple Pembina hills
licking his pains   ears pricked

     thin-pitched yips drop
the voice   an other answers—   hear
             I'm here

          a place to begin

apple pie & salsa

red & green, rotund & juicy
apple tart and tomato charm
    cheeky appeal

canning jars, rubber rings
bubbling baths
    sun-toil cheerity

apple butter, pie & sauce
fall-fresh pleasures
    sweet winter relish

tomato sauce, soup & salsa
hearty onion tears, piquant
    pepper-burnt fingers

sinus-clearing steam
gasps clasps potted
    arms embrace
    saucy kissed goodness

autumn's allure to conserve
    tongue-tangy treasures

sealing the harvest
in clear Kerr jars

it's not the cheer

it's not
fat-blossomed spring
draws my attention

nor the hot waves
whose husky voices
wash into
the sunburnt beach

it's not the frost
ferns that sprawl
on wintered windows

nor the blood-red
sun that bleeds
nocturnal lights

it's the cut-and-dried
fall fields that burst

the strong
orange pumpkins
those prairie pearls
those startled eyes

a yellow leaf

swings

from its perch

un

hinges

free-floater

skims

the surge

of sky

slaps

awake

grounded

into the blue

cool of now

white as mourning

nearly invisible
big-eyed on your pedestal
witness posted to the prairie pitch
you watch the winter faintly stir
white morning wind

a feathered wave

surprised to see you
rise & suppose
you may be the smile
on my snowcold face

light rails

spot-
       light   presses
       so thick and hot it burns
       rails into eyes locked open

piercing through
       the black curtain
       a glaring finger
       stabs and rips into my eyes
       stunned by the present
rays poke at days end
its nighted sighs and morning beam

OOOooooOOO...OOOooooOOO

miles and miles piled to this point
trail at the blinding
speed of sight splits
trebles in force traces
the dark veil erases
       luminosity yawns in elastic
       lines drawn across the rest
       -less prairied mindscape

=====tracks race on relentless==just beyond reach===

       where will you lay your blunted head
       and rest your worn-out wheels?
       your cracking heels laid to rust

             when pace of plains
             and nighted haze lift
             when ages alight
             and draw to arrest

now a days
train rails and
brain crossings track
for our time being

OOOooooo…OOOooooo…

=======till time loses track

watch the train

run across   the screen
the station schedules
the stationary   screen runs
the schedules   the station
your mind   the train
                     the time
to remember runs across
the screen   in seconds
                                in minutes
points out points
reference   referents
point to point   places it runs
refers to brain
              the train   to train
you to sit as you sit thinking
moving not moving
viewing the world
the world view   moving you
viewing you sitting
across the window screen
              windows
into time   the time it takes
to live from minute to minute
point to point you
point to your watch   turning
                           time
                           thinking

you watch your watch
watch the train move
as it moves across the screen it
          .   turns you

turns your mind in a moment
this moment time turns
on a point   a switch point
      the station
      the train
      the brain
      the time now switches
      the view points for you
            to remember
un-stationed   to run
                with the train

chuf-chum

CHUF chuf	CHUF chuf
CHUF chuf	CHUF chuf

steam-spits	rhythmics
loco-	motives
tempo-	prairies
whistle-full	scene-airy

CHUF chuf	CHUF chuf
CHUF chuf	CHUF chuf

convoy	rail-joy
black track	fast jack
chuf-tough	chug-a-long
Selkirk	loggin'-run

CHUF chuf	CHUF chuf
CHUF chuf	CHUF chuf

Hudson	CPR
prairie-pulse	resuscitate
CNR	*Mikado*
CAN-US	in/re-spire

CHUF chuf	CHUF chuf
CHUF chuf	CHUF chuf

plains-trains	steam-beat
motive-chant	obsolete
chuf-chug	chum-song
chum-hum	l-o-n-g-o-n-e

under the belt

      gone
is the sheen that once
girdled our home
gone the hay and the grain

from the groin of the earth
grave bones long for breath

they lie
cinched under the tree belt
voices rooted

bones beg sun's touch
tissues nerved

              sinew earth's bro
          -ken ribs renew by your everbreath
          figured from nether to everspring

        ... ...

mull our dry songs to bloodbrother wine

deadtothisworld bones burst into dancing
      unearthed a black belt of voices
            belting out blooms over pleated plains

if time

if time   then living is
& our dying must be
only the gardener
grooms the fruited tree

if time is not
            the gardener
ever greens trees
florid with praiseplums

if time-lessness is
self-lessness
then minds burn
bushes unconsumed
            taste
buds of memories
            & rememories
spring   free from haste
or fear of forgetting
            yellow-lobed pear
            redtart cranberry

no time is...
            all times being/being all times/
            times all being/times being all
                        fragrant
flourish but never fall
never wither only shine on all
            that is/lives

taste & see the allready
allways sunalive thrive
being in the evernow
          vivified stained glass
          colourwonder world
human brokenness heals
....born to unfold in hands

rainbows & angels take a bow
adore the lovergardener   touch
          the living dead

          trans
scented plantings
& everflowering in
-carnations   just as he said
death is treed & deracinated

if time's incantation meta-
morphs incalculable   then time falls
& heaven springs   humans blossom
breathe sun's untime

breathe

templed in ivory bone
breezes over
the crimson flesh-hold

whwhwhwhwh

h h h h h h

whwhwhwhwh

h h h h h h

b r e a t h e

h h h h h h o t
and wholly

scented breath in
-flows

lips
undone

tongues in
cheek bloom
          breathe

your word
my mouth

what lies

what lies behind
the lies we hide
behind   lies
we believe in

thinking we are un
lovable as the sun
chilling behind clouds
(un)wanted

fear of failure
our faces fracture
kernels that con
test germination

as if
forgiveness was
a foreign language
& ever-love never
breathed on earth

yet even rocks cry
against the lies
that grow in minds
like weeds

regarding division

"What does the camera lie about? Light divided by time.
A kiss cropped between truth and reproduction…"
—Méira Cook, *Slovenly Love*

click a slant of math, the camera /the kiss
a slant of mouth, a long following long
division photo re-vision = your oversight

light stands still. in cut time, splits then/now
yet neither, light a black & white yes
terday today replicating itself, exactly
a breathless lie thinly sliced

light flattens on photo
paper, death behind
still life a truth surfacing
chemically suggestive, image duplicates
itself preserved to forget depth *click*
the kiss: a moment of light
                     quick delight

yanked out of context *click* dis
located light shines backwards &
forwards torn
by exposure, framed. a darkroom
crime the photographer forges light
disregards what is hidden
a voyeur, covert, aims *click*
the aperture you peer through shudders
startles light & divides
                    /multiplies lies
                              the kiss
lights your incalculable eyes

33

she catches my eye

sinuous   in form her flight
light against the pewter film

she searches the surf
face   shining desire

        pterodactyl
                she hovers   between words
                                 between worlds

hers is the ageless sky black
waters her banquet table
        she flies
                alive from
                a white-on-black
                        movie across the screen   in slow
motion
      rises
           & falls ever so
                    slightly
                        a pen
                    -dant strung
                  from a pocket of air

raise your glass

the moon rises
　on the glass rim

　　　flying high I'm where
　　　　you shine beside sun
　　　stunned we ride
　　　　two sides of the glass

　　　light lives inside the gaps
　　　　pours between us
　　　pure vintage am I
　　　　your moon shine

　a reeling shadow or
your looking glass

spring

under a thick winter coat
she curls deep
                white & waiting
                thick with dreams

her thighs glisten in the sun's bright
                promises his smiles
she shivers

                longs for the runoff
                for the moment
when the cell of ice & snow crumbles
& the cold hand withdraws
                to gelid northern shoulders

crocuses
                crack the snow
                fling off linen gowns
                erupt along prairie
naked day murmurs mauve

her stiff winter coat
                                cast off
                earth jumps at the chance
                        to gloss the land

turn on the heat

heat activated
flames snap open
pop-ups in
a child's storybook

singeing winter's
bone cold
the wind-spun bulbs burn
to april extravagance

tulips
turn on the heat
carefree clowns
rousing clay
from their beds

a raucous menagerie
of circus performers

painted pomegranate red
& saffron yellow blow
their kisses sky-high

in the moment

you hear it heave
                snort & twitch
smell it brooding under the ice
                        spring
                under winter skin
                bulging to blisters

frosts forsake tree trunks
& the river rat clings to the banks
afraid to let go to & fro
            zen in the moment

                    a sharp tick
                    talks in contractions
                            the river screaks
                            its own contradictions

        wintered walls
        twist & roil & crush
                            spring boils over
board razing sand-bag
fences wrack your house
of cards flushed in the
            cataract moment

wasted voices

?? can you hear them

        tinkle under the ice
        ping the shores
        the weight of refuse

    gulls kick the coke can
dive beneath an oily brown
    face full of insect
    icides the acrid tides
    & stunted fish where mercury rises

plastics decorate the
    dead on arrival
    on the riverbed

geese screech
    gag on garbage
        eggs broken
        in glass & discarded newspapers
           diluted headlines declaim

           resources city wastes
           city wastes resources
           waste citys resources
           city resources wastes

      goslings beak out their shells
      peep to discover   feet
encrusted in managed excrement

I carry

laced round my neck
a charming miniature globe

others note its curved beauty
rich cobalt jade & sienna tones

this tiny world (un)rests my chest
pulses to tones that insinuate my voice

its circum-weight sways
back & forth along a gilded string

soft hymns of freedom
harmonies for all human(un)kind

neck laced I wear
(un)voice & (un)breath

what in the world do we mean
you mean the world to me

meanwhile it seems
I carry a ball & chain

pillowspeak & crowtricks

crows preen
    play as couples
    please the other
    peck behind ears
        whispering sweetsomethings

crows collect
    pretty things
    pocket away
    castoff swag
        junk for one   another's treasure

        do crows collect reasons
        or groom their passions?

somewhere down river
a woman throws bread
for a wild hungry goose
chases to catch the crust
        legend airy crows nearly
        human   naturally crafty
        their boffin tricks—living art

crow routes the goose mid
run drops a red maple leaf
    on the bread spread
        like strawberry jam
her peace ruffled
the daily bread
disappearing un
just

    she stands redblind
    unable to grasp the cawwws
    or know what it is
    the crow knows

raven beauty

struts along
smart-ass aristocrat
snappy in black tails

strides cross lanes
through paved plains against
the grain of traffic
& agog forest fields

fearless he raves
of distant flights
& foreign sights
crows of rare tales
uncommon travails
the heavy crown he wears

the raven beauty
scavenges on
the calamities of others

avidly picks his menu
from the black top

what crow

black as a top hat perched
in the crook of a leafless limb
he guffaws at the world
beneath him

the crow
& gulls   overhead
            one
            lets it fly
through the air
the aim
            remarkable
            impeccable

shot
            between
            their coupled hands
                        shit
                        hit
(not the fan)
/her bare toes

            squawk squark yawp caw
            he jaws with delight

fowl droppings splatter the pair
            should've seen it comin

what the crow
said · screeching
                        / sniggering

till the wind
clawed
his throat

you did it again

you did it again
put it up there
out there for all
to see your half
moon face at sea

I see you at it
up there planting
a thumb print
in dusky clay your
red impression

inside night you
pose as though
you own up to
your pale face
—now you've gone

& done it again odd
-acious & full-faced
from your berth blowing
places open on the moor

eyes buoyed
by your bright phase

a smudge

moon traverses our sleepless path
    tentative at this outrageous hour
        5 a m

its stain rubbed out of sight upon our return
    eye/witnesses an ambitious orange
        rose a sun

in motley rays rides among
    darkened trees springs & touches
        our shadows

bear witness to the smudge of time taken
    to stir moon into sun

the hunt

it stalks
      in silence
                waiting
for the moment

it creeps
     in

on uncertainties

a snap of light
        springs

from the shadows

     seizes
        the black & white plot

    black imprints
       on a white leaf

he is not here

not
where I expected him

    leaving me here
    an empty day

empty except for his shirt
        lying
    neatly on the bed

light streams dustily
      from the entrance
      white walls washed

there are no portraits

    framed
    & hung

            he is
            not here

lunar tides

the breast of your light
leans against my bruised ribs

against the silent
chill that wafts shadow

heart mindbent queries
ebb & flow along shorelines

each time you sing love in white
unmeasured tides

would you

like to sit along
that wall or in the far corner
by the window

    she chooses a table for two
    blooming in sun

organic as the potted tree behind her
the menu sprouts
green on the pages
The Dandelion Eatery

he fills her glass
a swash of cool
water spills his smile
       todays special
       yam soup with corn a touch of garlic
       cilantro and coconut milk

brown hair splashed with silver-blond
wisps cascade over his rain-blue eyes
       expectant
              she leans
in the arms of her
chair would you like
       coffee
   please
          curls from the corner
            of her lips
brows flirt   turn
pages dreaming
the company of another
         drawn
to the line
   of box cars
left to right

the train
        reads   slow
across   the windowed gaze
the tug and tone of city
strings   locomotive & poet
playing the moment

he sings coffee
more coffee
      would you

the rich café in antiphony swirls
cursive in the cup of her ears
sits sipping sun through an hourglass

      his face emerges
light   as a story
blue saucer eyes
communing
coffee cups chime
at the tangerine table
     for two

the metro train
calls a spray
of gilded tones fall
in love among metered lines

would you
would you please me
    & read me
    coffee warm
    in your time

when i read you

when i read you
i want to let go

drawn under
by the heat   your skin
your pulse
in sync sinking
into mine

open to your whims
your touch
goose bumps
along my spine

your mouth i want
my tongue
you turning my sheets
touching every naked
move my body makes

fill the white
with your longings
hold me while
i read you over & over
& all over me

reading lamp

planted for hours at my desk I peruse
dark paths of language
knotted roots of old scripts

old man
          u-script-marshes stagnate
leaves of forgotten tree-lines
every october unread   de-compose

stumble through the woods of prose
thickets of the said & un-said
sad thoughts in mis-reading(s) felled &
pressed onto a million pages

worming through words phase by phrase
a single lamp opens
lightens & re-paginates   I step
towards a word that might tell
the woodland of his story

the corner chair

invitations
on the small
soft chair that leans against
the wall robed in
a daylily yellow
sunrays spill the window

petite arms
enfold not one
    but two
lovers drawn deep into each

beneath the bookshelf edge
   laid back and expectant
content to read
me into your eyes
romancing the tome
romancing me

we glide on cloud ninety
-nine to scan purple
hills & puffed-up prairie skies spy
on the gods the beasts the giants
green in our hands

strange scholar bound to be a voyeur con
joined in ecstasies
  with you dear
reader now in this corner
chair wrapped inside or under
your soft freshly laundered covers

the curve rains deep

how deep
the curve from me to you
& does the bend change when moving
the line from you to me amend the distance

the pitch we know modulates
when we meet
eyes shift the curve you throw
me in sudden proximity

cursively we move
along the bends & turns
arcing each toward each
compelled by lines we have drawn

so close we can touch the rim
feel rain
pervious as a cloud
our previous faces dip &
carve our dreams

this strange curvature
you & me

bent nearly
out of shape

you are...

the slice of sun   the rim of night
crocus   in mauve mind   blizzard-busy

in january haze
a clearing a doubt-full forest

spill your coffee-comfort down my spine
   fill the chill of my cup to the ken

                you are
always now   my breathing room
when yesterdays fall
                        one by one
steadily off
                the Steinbach Credit
Union calendar

behind the door

what lies behind
the sun-bleached
door
       rusty-hinged
       & locked
padlocked in fact

       as though
the world inside
might come unhinged
         escape too monstrous
            too risqué
            the binge

worn slats
strain to breaking
       what lies
          beyond
the paint-chipped
panels   imagine
         the heft

     of wonder
     or worry
that drubs & roils
behind the door

       the potent breach
       of secrecy

lay me down

now I
      lay
            me down
                to sleep

            & pray
I'll find
      you
            when I
                wake

to lie with
      out is cold
      & dead de-
light
                the lack

      as children pray
   together forever family

      lay me down
                to sleep
      while he wanders

         love
            a
           wake

black & white

stealing from room
        to room she slides
silent as a hot blade
through butter
        moon melts
        on the floor

black then back then
black & white blocks
        she carries
                the words
        through sleep
less night

dissolving carpet
        moon flees the sun
slicing open day
engraving black then white then
black & white the words
        unconstrained she carves

you don't get it

alone in this house emptied
all of love I love only my bones
hung together on a ridge
this purple moor hard & brittle
stones carried in a craggy skin-bag

there is no man waiting to hold
me in his warmth no lover
to touch me to sleep or set
breakfast in the early blue of day
you think I don't remember
        skin or tongue

savouring the cool of our salad
      we mum & nibble
they say greens keep things
regular like the ground-in habits
keep me steady anchored while cracks
form between folded calendars

your books hold secret conversations
your eyes I long to read my way to but
there's no competing with *Wuthering* Emily
nor the patter of talk
      property taxes are up   *my hairdresser found*
      God   *mice*   *in the teatowel*
      drawer   *Shirley died*   *of cancer*
sounds like someone else

or pickled like your pimento damn Law
      the psycho therapy   *isn't helping*
words fall off my tongue
ice cubes cracking glass

me at the kitchen
table choking on pain &
unripe melon
swallowed in the incessant
wind & rain

blue moon daze

your once
-in-a-blue-moon gaze
bold &

mine to hold

your dubious
volte-face

blur the verge
con
verse to some
other
moon

by deg
-rees
you
turn
burn
by day
to light

nothing personal
you say   poker-faced

when night
suddenly dawns
on me

time will tell

time will tell to
morrow's secrets
spot endings & fresh starts
from time to time
clouds deny or dole out

time will tell   will you
be early or late or
on the dot just in time
to show & tell   will you re
turn or kill time   time will
tell yesterday has left
a stain on time
will tell the day
you left

what do you
tell time

there is not enough
or too much and
how to tell time

did you leave
the key

time will tell
what happens
what happens
when time tells

I am not
the same as
I yester
day was

never enough
time to touch
the horizon neither
time nor cease to wink

to think
we have moved

weather wears

we had weather again
today whether (or not)
the forecasters got it right

weather takes life in
to its own hands carries
time clinking in bottled air

the colour of wind colours our eyes
whether they are open (or not)
lungs in & out of season

cold that heat outlasts
weathering wherever we go
our calling matters

whether you know it (or not)
one moment melts the next
wearing down the awares we wear
wherever weather happens

undone

                                                    open mags
                                          or tomes from the back
                                          side scan the pages
                                                  till eyes trip
                                                 on a line____
                                              or snag a word
                                              wool on a nail
                                          a s t r a n d pulled
                                    from a favourite sweater
                              u n r a v e l l i n g
                        t h e   s l e e v e s
a skein
of yarn loops
in warp & weft knit
        to my eyes
round my needled mind
pointed verses   converse
        purl   & cast off
threads till I've come
undone strand by
strand stand back
to front
                        back to the beginning
                          naked & lost
                          & found
                                          bound by the sound
                                          fibres of every word
                                          doubly knit

read red

when i read

     red on the edge
               sun basking
        eyes on
           dusk

     or the spiralling
               candy-cane stripes
        sweet sense
           on tongue

     the red rush
          unhinges
               bellies & faces

     caramel-coated
               circus &
               campfire choruses

     sudden flush
               blood-orange
               fruit of passion

i read red

when i read red
        i read you

well woman

well woman
is it a wishing well
what do you   really want

you think your wish
will be quenched if
          you keep coming
back   to this
          well enough

you've tried many
wells & still
          you remain
          looking for water

from how many
          wells
will you sip

          drink & drink &
          drink again but
          never full
          -filled

I know where you've been
& the wells you've seen
          drawn your need to
          drawn to your need

          consider this
          you ought not resist
          woman a well
          that never runs dry

            the well
you seek woman
well   I am he
wishing you well

a-lone

a-lone, I am not
though skies flush and fade
coffee-ers sip
over crinching bags
and kwooshing machines
the steady zip of waiters
quicker than zippers

all-one I am
blinking through dirty panes
study autos flizz by to home
gaping absence of some-one

a-lone, but not
I wanting to say
eyes caught between lines
author-friend reminds me
of the you I failed to see

alone, with you
aware of you still
sudden smell of
coffee   you
at home
inside me

mourning air

coooOOOoo ooo oo
coooOOOoo ooo oo oo

why do you   sing
such songs as the sun
shoos away night
might you be mourning
your younglings grown

shaken off their shells
and flown the coop
come to love the sites
on their own

coooOOOoo ooo oo

emptynesting the tree
house swept clean except
for silent chirps &
a chipped cup

mourn in remembrance
their dark trusty eyes
their fears of flying ousted

mourn
their bonethin wings
& gawky heads smitten
with prairiewide skies

meno madness

how do you do
      meno   pause   your imbalance
      hormones all heyday
fight
        to con   troll the game
                          live play
                          m-bodied craze
meno
pause   a gap that sputters
        be   tween   spark
                           & plug
out of gas
              exhausted
                  you spout anger
hic   coughs   stutters
your glottis makes
              glutinous tongue
                  still speech
less spas
        modic i reg u lar ity mal
        func tion ing san ity
              de ranged   no   room
                           to   roam in
                           sanity un sound

out of mind   off the element   foolish
                                 reason
        on the hot seat
we all folly down
drown
        under heat waves   a flash in the pan   dis
                              ordered   dysthymia

hard to swallow
climacteric   flares
                    blood thinner   middle thicker
                                         hair whiter
                                                    legs stiffer

what it is to meet
to splay & percolate

newsflash

headlines abuzz today again
pain to reign in her skull
hair from the roots
threatening to knock out the back
door of her midlifeyes

imagine a cell where no light
or pleasure penetrates where
breath is stolen the head
room squeezed & vise
gripped in a flash
of heat that puts
the entire body into seizure

       unable to find or hold
her head prickles skin glistens she listens
laughter ping pongs across cafe tables
to traffic cables drawn on the other side
held in custody she awaits bail &
the breaking of her prison-moment
                        news hotflash:

       painkiller springs her from the headhold
       eyelids swing open fall in line with the green
       balloons bopping to a young boy's walk
       his t-shirt flashes lemonyellow light dis
       -charges in her dark headroom a snap
       shot out of the blue—acquittal   at last
           sun shines sheer

the worth of a woman

what is

the worth of a woman
:when her children have opened and shut
child-rooms to worlds of their own

:when the fire-works of hormones burst
across another scattered night

:when her breasts slump and beauty slides
into wrinkles   fat   and lizard skin

what is

the worth of a woman
:when the phone sleeps and the coffee spoon
lies on the cold kitchen table

:when her memory limps along the scrim of dusk
wrapped in the gauzing years

:when laughter chokes on sickly phlegm
and zwieback crumbs of grief

by the time you learn to love life
your flesh peels from the bones

so what

what is her worth

island

so woman is but man is not an island seaing as Istand alone
on thisland perhaps a woman who longs to live
inland hand inhand with an/other 'tis safer holdinhands
is what I've been told it's warmer when you
have a companion island someone in mind and when two
are gathered there he is yet here is where Istand a lone isle
landed in midst of the plains how much more inland
than Winnipeg I-landed because I co-own a house and a back
yard (is)landing because my grandparents came to thisland
from Ukraine in breach of I-landed because I'm an isle stranded
uncertain where to go fearing I'll drown in sight of inside of land
in reach of reaching a hand for another isle or could Iunland and
swim the prairies to discover new I's other I's stranded hands out
stretched as Iland further inland to reland with another isle
two I's oversea ourland hands on and Iland my hands on you

back these bare bones

you take me by your hands
make no bones about it
run fingers along my back
for the joy of hearing it crack

*don't step on a crack
you'll break your mother's back*

your hands hurt
make no bones about it
bringing into line my bended spine
one vertebra at a time until
body fits desire's shape

your hands re-locate
my funny bones and activate
the humours of my temperament
urge back bones into alignment
reposition and reframe me   *snap crackle pop*
oh my benefactor and my chiropractor   *Kyrie Eliason*

*sticks and stones may break my bones
but words will* bend and mend me

so make new bones about it
give me your hands
these bare-bone words
underwrite my undercarriage
delete loose sticks, rework stones
realign and mend my broken tale
and make new bones about it

life-drops

life-drops leafing
        fall
          ing
with age
seasoned bits
     shift
         turn
           & settle
spent

mounds of remembered sun
insects in hidden regret

missed opportunities etched into
         time-lines
    life
      drops
            bit
           by
        bit
     weather bitten

red rivers

damned red   out of the blue
a backlog of river
      shudders under pressure
      snatches breath gone
      into thin air

limbs numb   succumb to the attack
time cut into pieces   of pain

blood locked behind bars (the door
jam)   hammers
      the body defence
less red a shade of blue
      his off
            beat heart
dying to inhale   the pulse
      of red rivers

we a clod

aging   l i n e s & pol-ka-spots
the sag
       & rag   of a lifetime

time's a sling   shot
                we a clod
                     r o l l i n g a w a y
feet first

               reeling in the family   l i n e
like a rod   s t r u n g o u t
      fishing
      for something just
some thing
fair &
square
     till the f l a t l i n e___^__^_____^_____

                       catches
our surprise

in stitches

laughter bumps along
the hallways
straining to hold a heart
she adjusts her body
in sheets smelling of hospital
careful to keep tubes
from tangling or exposing
her limp pale skin

                her head
flops on the white pillow
a giddy child or drunk
old man the woman drifts in
and out of where we wait

when no one is watching
will caress with care
the tender spot incised by the blade
the wild cells preying on her mind
flesh praying for laughter of
great-grandchildren she hopes
yet to hold
in stitches

terminal

pa-bumm pa-bumm pa-bumm pa
beeeeeeeeeeeee

she arrives at the terminal
steady life-beat hooked
on the eye of hesitation
      a blink
      a breath   snatches
& vanishes
      leaving an emptied line
      a body self less
      & mourners in the hospital room

          we are double
          -born spirited
          & terminal

      no other options
      no returns
      no exchanges
      no operations
alter the prognosis

terminal at every turn
our passage here is not forever
      passengers of time
      pulsing till the clock stops
          on a point
of conversion
      re-location
          a transferral
          counter clock
wise one limb
      spun on
          to a new branch

                    terminal
pa-bumm pa-bumm pa
our being
                    spirit-borne
                    pneuma we are old
and newly mothered

the dark way

there is a nowhere
place of prayer only
you can't really pray
there where
words whack
an ethereal wall
you know exists

God seems not
to have arrived
& you grieve though
no death has occurred
yet weary you wait
as if for a train
that fails to arrive

you wait   on hold
there without
music to mollify
your ears

blindly you wander
in limbo balloon words
bobbing on ceilings
going nowhere   you
have no recourse
but to pass the wall

down the dark way
to the light side
walking alone by prayer

light promises

fear sitting next to you
the fire burns your breath

catches me on a blade
of grass bursting to flame

lapsed promises light
an instant then burn black

the stem crumples to ashes
choking my blue lungs

where is the soul match
of ever-after promises?

love's flame
that never dies in
the cold ground?

the word
that never
burns
out

the dark side of God

taciturn i stir the dark
side of God fumble
stumble over silence
fearing exposure
though wrapped in
the umbrous robe
of his night

the box in my chest thumps
against its shuttered latch

to speak   or not
is that a question
what good are words
when he knows   or does he
want to hear me
click open the terrible treasures
lift out the secret shadows i feel
guilt blues & black
hurts sparring
a brawl in my chains

bawling unleashes the pain
constrained in the dark
room heart wedged
open i shout
till the box is still

linger strangely warmed
in his invisible bright

here on your side i
feel the light in your dark
shades of me brighten
by your darkness the shadow
box lightens   dissolves
within your ribs
un-guilted i touch
your dark side
word breathed
& safe

dream works

what is a dream
        without a revelation
                an angel
        without a message

reassurance of these
                in/sights
        you desire
                to verify

feel the dream
        solid as the table
        that bears your book

                exposé as audible
        as the voice
you hear on the radio
promise of rain tomorrow

in one ear & out
                song in/sight

        imagine the faces
        you cannot see
fall against sound

on other side of dream
air & water
        zygotic
                revelations trans
                scribed in/tangible letters

caesarian

you say   I must aim
                  for the caesura
        drive   to the end
        of the line & then   stop

                  female desire
                  this live wire   body
craves
a language re-born
            new ways to play
            the breast & babble
                        loose
                tongue arrested

materials in hand
            my pen knife marks
            the caesarian line
                    the great   divide

between you   &   me

you cut the surface   expectant
            tear through tissue   placental
            surgically extract
                the issues   natal   gifts

            I slide along the crease
            & stretch beyond the lines   birth
                                  marked

        carved
for bearing

toe the line

tip   toe   a   long   the   centre
   line where the standard
tears & tugs
     a war between
   convention & mutiny

   out of
     line
fingers ache from head
to toe the line
    it self un
     done

hold the line un
fold the tangled
   blue prints
        that wash
   in waves
against
   your feet doubling
        over
     so difficult to con
form to standard
pattern that waves
like an ensign

     tug
    & turn down
       the centre tip

   toe
     a bout the spit   of sand
       the shift
         ting hand

why come back

why do you
        like
        me
come
     keep coming
back   to the line
this line   of ecstasy
this line of thought
     when it comes
         up
    comes
        down
the line   limps
     feet shift
     tongue fumbles
for the right
       words
you falter
     break
        your line
of thought
     vacillate
       its late
are you going
        or coming

back
     to the line
the sheer pleasure of

the lame and the halt

an end

              to begin
              at the end
of the line emptied &
desperate for what??
          (the blank you fill)

          for a second take
                      look

the trail does not stop
veers to the right
          (or left)
                    open
     again
              to begin

take one
          you throw
                    a sneer in tomorrow's face
                    smear possibility against
                              today's wall

                              a dead end end

          your view you bend again
steer   to the left
                              right
                                   look
     a gain
          the second take

                                   an end alive

                    again

to begin

whispers of grace

the old rhythms of sleep
        inhale   exhale
              in & out

each breath
                you warm
                against my skin

feel weight of dawn find its way
behind curtained eyelids

                listen
to your breath
where daylight enters

                morning is not
                a guarantee

    but for you & me
                we'll have our toast
                & cereal prayers

the highest praise

in the park a guitar strums
he comes unannounced

kneels to the soul song
dark dreadlocks sway

to the lonely street beat
homeless & holy he sings

one spirit   one creator

eyes closed he's oblivious
to the gathering crowd

hearts nod to the healer
hallelujah is the highest praise

ears & tears string strangers
together blur black & white

light draws incense into dark days
praise the colour of antiphony

        clap your tiny hands
their soulful tongues attune

hallelujah is the highest praise
hallelujah is the highest praise

notes & acknowledgements:

Thanks to my creative writing teachers and poets who have read my words, and whose classes or seminars have enriched my writing: Brenda Austin-Smith, Dennis Cooley, Robert Kroetsch, Méira Cook, Alison Calder, David Arnason, Lorna Crozier, Jennifer Still, Angeline Schellenberg, Erin Mouré, Catherine Hunter, Sally Ito, Sue Goyette, Katherena Vermette … …

Special thanks to my writers' group for their perceptive readings and encouragements: Gerry Wolfram, Brenda Sciberras, and Jim Anderson.

Thank you Jamis Paulson for the beautiful cover design; thanks also to Sharon Caseburg and everyone at Turnstone Press for their careful attention to this manuscript.

My gratitude and admiration go to Dennis Cooley for his generous support and insightful editing.

I am honoured to include an epigraph taken from *Slovenly Love* by Méira Cook (Brick Books 2003, 96), used with her permission.

Versions of several poems have appeared previously in *Rhubarb* magazine; thanks to executive editor Victor Enns and poetry editor Di Brandt.

I wish to acknowledge the influence of Struan Sinclair's *Automatic World* (Doubleday 2009) in "watch the train"; Anne Carson's "The Glass Essay" (*Glass, Irony & God*, New Directions 1995) in "you don't get it."

Thanks to my mentors, cheerleaders, co-workers, and coffee-ers who believed in me, even when I didn't believe in myself.

Countless thanks belong to my children Kevin, Kristin, Kerri and their families, my parents Allen and Betty, my extended family, and most of all to Terry, whose support and love live behind the words of these poems.